In This Proud Land

THE STORY OF A MEXICAN AMERICAN FAMILY

Bernard Wolf

B. Lippincott Company / Philadelphia and New York

Many fine people made this book a reality by giving the author their time, concern, and involved assistance: Dorothy Briley, Jean Krulis, and Carlos Crosbie of J. B. Lippincott Company; Sara Ishikawa and Alex Zermeno of Berkeley, California; Raul Yzaquirre, national director, National Council of La Raza, Washington, D.C.; Gus Guerra, superintendent of schools (and a most remarkable man), Pharr–San Juan–Alamo Independent School District, Pharr, Texas; Jesse Vela, Jr., Title One migrant evaluator, PSJA Independent School District, Pharr, Texas; John McKeever, principal, PSJA High School, Pharr, Texas; Rosalinda Trevino, community aide, PSJA High School, Pharr, Texas; Alex Moreno, director, Colonias del Valle, San Juan, Texas; Larry Sing, migrant field agricultural agent, American Crystal Sugar Company, Minnesota; the Wiese family of Halstad, Minnesota; and, once again, Mike Levins, who prepared the outstanding photographic prints for this book. To all of these and to the many others who helped, the author is truly indebted.

U.S. Library of Congress Cataloging in Publication Data

Wolf, Bernard.
In this proud land.
SUMMARY: Portrays the arduous life of a large Mexican American family, residents of the Rio Grande Valley in south Texas, who migrate yearly to northern states to do farm work.
1. Mexican Americans—Rio Grande Valley—Social conditions—Juvenile literature. 2. Rio Grande Valley—Social conditions—Juvenile literature. [1. Mexican Americans—Texas. 2. Rio Grande Valley—Social conditions. 3. Migrant labor] I. Title.
F392.R5W64   976.4'4'0046872   78-9680   ISBN-0-397-31815-4

With profound admiration for the
Hernandez family,
and for all those who struggle with dignity

The Rio Grande Valley is a land proud of its achievements. Until the early years of this century, it was mostly arid brush country, inhabited by poor Mexican farmers and some Indians. In 1915, the first white settlers arrived, attracted by the low cost of land, cheap labor, and the irrigation potential of the Rio Grande river.

At the same time, Mexico was undergoing a period of major revolutionary upheaval. Bands of outlaws led by men like Pancho Villa crossed the river border to raid the herds and crops of the new Anglo settlers. Because of the shifting course of the Rio Grande, border disputes were frequent, and they often led to violent solutions. An atmosphere of mutual distrust arose between the Anglos and the Mexicans. Every man carried a gun, and shootings for real or imagined provocations were not uncommon.

In order to relieve overpopulation and defuse political tensions in Mexico, the Mexican government began to encourage its poor and desperate masses to migrate north into Texas. The Americans agreed to this plan. Soon thousands of Mexican families crossed the border as *braceros*—"arm" laborers who worked for very little money on the large farms and ranches of the Anglos. Gradually, a "live and let live" attitude was established between America and Mexico. Tensions subsided, and the Anglo settlers could now turn their undivided energies to developing the rich promise of their newly acquired land.

Today, the Rio Grande Valley is one of the most productive agricultural regions in the United States. The great river has been harnessed to provide a constant supply of water. That, combined with the warm climate and flat terrain, makes possible all-year harvests of a variety of vegetables and citrus fruits.

The majority of the Valley's residents are Mexican Americans. While relations between the Anglo and Mexican American communities are not always cordial, they are at least courteous. For those who own the land, the Valley is a prosperous place. But those who work in the fields often have hard lives.

Mexican Americans who live in the Valley find it hard to obtain steady farm work. When they can get work, the going rate of pay is $2.65 an hour. But many farmers prefer to hire Mexican "wetbacks" who cross the border illegally and without work permits. These people are willing to work for only $1.50 an hour. In addition, modern machinery has replaced many workers formerly required to harvest certain crops. As a result, thousands of Mexican American families must leave the valley each spring to seek employment as migrant farm workers in northern states.

Yet, despite all odds, Mexicans in lartge numbers continue to depart from their homeland and enter south Texas as legal immigrants. Most speak no English, have little money, and are poorly educated. Those who do not have friends or relatives in the Valley soon find themselves forced to live in *colonias*—squalid shantytowns that stretch from one end of the Valley to the other in an unrelenting chain of human misery. In the *colonias* there are no paved roads, and often there is no electricity. The land has no drainage facilities—when it rains, the ground becomes a sea of mud. There is no inside plumbing. Frequently the only water available for drinking, cooking, and washing must be carried in buckets from nearby irrigation canals. Tuberculosis and dysentery are common diseases among the residents.

Everyone looks for work, but jobs are scarce. Welfare is all too often the only way to survive. For those who are proud, such a solution is demoralizing. Many men abandon their families because they cannot find work to support them.

In the *colonias,* it is the children who suffer the most. However, if a child can survive disease, malnutrition, and the scars of a broken family, this is where hope for the future lies. Some families stay together. Some manage to leave the *colonias* and move the next step up the ladder from poverty.

Only ten short miles separate the Hernandez family from the Mexican border and their past. They live in the town of Pharr, Texas. While the distance from Mexico is small, they have come a long way in their struggle to better their lives. Like many Mexican Americans who live in the Valley, they are devout Catholics who get great comfort and spiritual support from their religion.

Father O'Malley is deeply loved by his Mexican American congregation at Saint Anne's Church. Sometimes they tease him gently about his pronunciation, but they are genuinely grateful and moved each Sunday morning when he conducts High Mass in Spanish and administers Holy Communion. The mystery and the majesty of the ritual never fail to refresh the spirits of the Hernandez family.

David Hernandez is forty-five years old. He is soft-spoken and never raises his voice in anger. He loves to tell jokes and make people laugh. But beneath his easygoing manner lie quiet stubbornness and determination. In his own unassuming way, he is a proud man who has much to be proud of.

Maria de los Angeles Hernandez is a strong, handsome woman with a passion for all growing things—the plants in her backyard, young animals, and, especially, her seven children.

Mr. and Mrs. Hernandez first met at a dance in their hometown, Linares, Mexico. She was impressed by his skill as a dancer and his lively good humor. He was struck by her slender beauty and warmhearted common sense.

The years that followed their marriage were full of hardship and sacrifice for the young couple. They lived in and around the town of Reynosa, near the American border, moving from one shabby shack to another while they worked for various farmers. Between them, they could earn no more than the equivalent of $5 to $7 a week to support their growing family. After thirteen difficult years, the family was finally granted U.S. immigrant status in 1969.

Neither Mr. nor Mrs. Hernandez speaks, reads, or writes any English. They feel they are too old now to learn such a complicated new language. But they are giving their children a great gift—the desire for better education and a talent for celebrating life one day at a time.

There are six girls and one boy in the Hernandez family. Five of the girls live at home with their parents. Oralia, who is twenty-one, is married and lives in a nearby town. She comes to visit her family almost every day. Her brother, Lazaro, is twenty-two. He is away on a scholarship at the University of Michigan, where he is preparing to enter the School of Architecture.

Mrs. Hernandez's mother, Castula Salazar, helps her granddaughters make tamales. It's hot in the house, but no one minds. The small kitchen comes alive with happy laughter and good-natured teasing. The tamales consist of dried corn leaves stuffed with a mixture of *masa*—cornmeal—ground pork, cumin, black pepper, salt, lard, and chopped onion. Grandmother Castula expertly folds the corn-husk wrappings and Mrs. Hernandez steams the tamales until their fragrance fills the house. When they are done, she gives some to her mother and another batch to Oralia to take to her husband. No one ever leaves her house with an empty stomach or with empty hands.

Mr. Hernandez is a carpenter's assistant. He works for an independent small building contractor. For the past three weeks, he and three other men have been building a one-family house in the town of Edinburg, about eight miles from Pharr. It will take another three weeks to finish this small home, which will sell for $24,000—a price far beyond the combined means of Mr. Hernandez and his co-workers.

When David Hernandez lived in Mexico, he was apprenticed to a bricklayer. He found he had an aptitude for construction work. It was this line of work that helped him and his wife realize their dream of emigrating to the United States. A carpenter who lived in Pharr agreed to hire him and train him to do carpentry. This man also furnished him with a letter of sponsorship, guaranteeing that he would have employment and not be a burden to the state. Only then could the Hernandez family obtain U.S. immigrant status and Mexican passports.

David Hernandez earns an average of $87 a week—when there is work. Last year he made about $2,000 on construction jobs. This is not nearly enough money to support his family. Because of the high cost of building materials and the competition for contracts in the Valley, his boss feels he cannot pay Mr. Hernandez more and still make a reasonable profit. There are larger construction firms that pay higher wages, but these companies prefer to hire younger men with specialized skills. They also want men who speak fluent English. So, each spring, David Hernandez must close up his house and take his family north to earn additional income. He is still a *bracero*.

For the past six years, Mr. Hernandez and his family have spent their summers working for the same farmer in Michigan. As long as the asparagus crop was good, there was steady work and income. Last year, as migrant farm workers, he and his family earned $4,000. But that year the asparagus fields yielded poorly, and Mr. Hernandez was told there would be no work the following season. Now, although it is only mid-February, he is concerned about the summer to come.

The average income of a Mexican American family in the Valley, with all family members working, is $4,000 a year—far below the national poverty level. The Hernandezes are not as poor as some, but Mr. Hernandez knows that if his family does not find summer work, they will be in deep financial trouble. He has already begun asking *compadres* if they know of any farmers up north who might hire extra workers this year.

At twenty-four, Rosa Martha is a beautiful, sensitive young woman who finds herself torn between conflicting realities. Because she is the eldest of the Hernandez children, she remembers most vividly the harshness and anxiety of her parents' life in Mexico. Before the family moved to Pharr, she completed her first year at a university in Mexico. Her ambition was to become a teacher. But once the family was settled in the Valley, they needed money urgently, and so she went to work.

Rosa Martha works as a seamstress in a shirt factory in McAllen. She is a skillful worker, and was recently offered a promotion to production supervisor, which would have meant an increase in salary. She decided not to accept the promotion because, as a supervisor, she would have to "overlook" many things she does not like about working conditions at the factory. Many of the women employed there are illegal aliens who come across the border each morning and return to Mexico in the evening. The illegal workers are paid far less than other workers,

and Rosa Martha does not want to be the kind of boss who participates in unfair and illegal employment practices.

Rosa Martha's take-home pay is $78 a week. She gives $40 to her mother for family expenses and $2 each to her three youngest sisters for pocket money. She uses some of what is left for personal needs. The rest she spends on such things as material from which to make clothes for herself and her sisters. Next to food, clothing is one of the family's main expenses. Fortunately, the Hernandez girls are rather evenly matched in height and size, so there is always a friendly exchange of their combined wardrobe.

Rosa Martha is still not comfortable with the English language. For three years, she has been enrolled in a basic adult course in English to get the practice she needs. The class meets two nights a week at an elementary school in Pharr. Her teacher, Mr. Guerra, insists that all questions and answers be given in English. He asks his students to correct one another's errors and encourages them to laugh together

over their mistakes, instead of feeling self-conscious about them. He has been urging Rosa Martha to apply for a scholarship to Pan American University in nearby Edinburg. Rosa Martha still longs to become a teacher. But how, she wonders, will her family manage without her financial help?

Oralia, the third oldest Hernandez child, shares her mother's great love for children and expresses it in a very special way. During the past two years she has worked with trainable mentally retarded children as a teacher's aide.

Each weekday morning at seven Oralia drives to her job at Edison Elementary School in Pharr. Miss Gorena, the teacher she assists, has worked with mentally retarded children for fifteen years. She says she has never married because she needs no children other than the ones she cares for and helps every day.

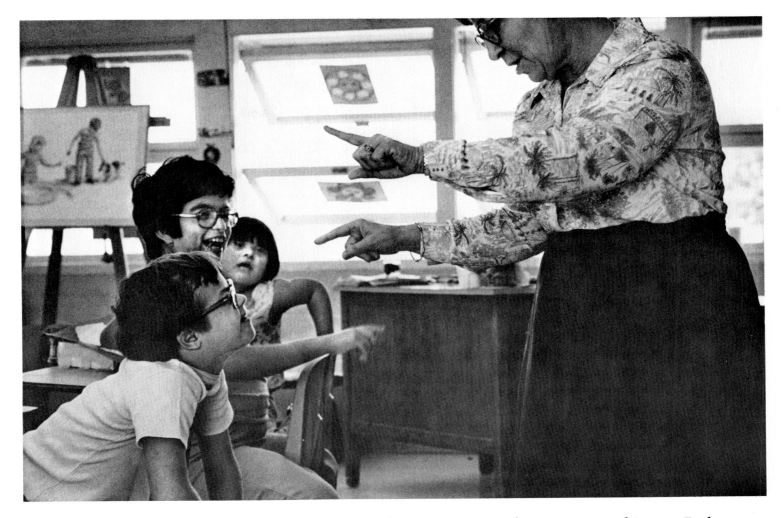

The children in Miss Gorena's class range in age from seven to thirteen. Each requires special training and encouragement. Sometimes a child needs to be taught such basic things as how to bathe and dress. A child may even have to be taught how to speak. Despite the fact that skeptical educators say she will never get anywhere, Miss Gorena teaches her students standard school subjects like reading, writing, and arithmetic. Not only are the children learning, they are also enjoying the challenge.

Until the mid-1960s, public education was not readily available to the children of migrant workers. There were attendance requirements that children who moved frequently could not meet. When Congress ruled that school districts that did not provide educational services for migrant students would not be eligible for federal aid to education, the situation changed dramatically. Now children who might never have attended school are getting an education in schools that have adapted to the migrant way of life.

The Hernandez children are among those who benefit from improved educational opportunities. Maria, nineteen, is a senior at Pharr—San Juan—Alamo (PSJA) High. Maria wants to enter the field of business administration, and most of her courses focus on business skills. She is learning to operate office machines, take shorthand, and do bookkeeping. She wants to attend Pan Am University in the fall, and hopes to qualify for a scholarship.

English is one of the most important subjects migrant students study. Most speak only Spanish at home and with their friends because it is more comfortable to do so. However, they must be able to express themselves clearly and easily in English if they wish to go on to college and find well-paid careers.

Maria's teacher of Mexican American history wants his students to gain an appreciation for their cultural heritage, so, today, they will make tortillas. These are the Mexicans' form of bread, and the skill required to make them could easily be lost. The cornmeal dough is shaped into small balls and rolled into round, flat pancakes that can't be too thick or too thin. To everyone's surprise, one of the boys rolls the best tortillas of all. After the tortillas are toasted, the students fill them with refried beans, chili sauce, and guacamole—a mashed avocado salad with finely chopped chili peppers and spices.

Maria's last class ends at midday. She goes to the school's parking lot, where she has left the family van. Public transportation is practically nonexistent in Pharr, and most people learn to drive when they are very young. The van is the only vehicle the Hernandezes own. It has seen many years of hard use in the Valley and during the family's annual migrations to the north. It demands frequent repair and coddling, and it consumes a great deal of fuel. Maria must pay for the gasoline out of her own money. Now, she finds she has flooded the engine and the van won't start. She pokes around under the hood and finally coaxes the motor into action.

Maria arrives home at one o'clock. She works on her school assignments until two-forty-five. Then it is time to drive to nearby Alamo, where she has a steady part-time job.

During the last eight months, Maria has worked for the Valley Truck Parts and Services Company, a firm that repairs diesel-powered container trucks. At the end of the week, after Social Security deductions, her take-home pay is $28. Half of that goes to her mother for family expenses.

Maria's duties range from answering the telephone, relaying messages, typing letters, and doing billing, bookkeeping, accounting, and the payroll, to picking up and delivering parts. Her workday ends at six P.M., but she frequently works much later. Good part-time jobs are hard to find in the Valley. Maria was only able to get this one because of her excellent work and grades in her vocational courses at school.

Margarita is eighteen, a year younger than Maria. She is a sophomore at PSJA High School. She attends the afternoon session —her first class begins at twelve-twenty.

This morning, after waking up unusually late, Margarita isn't feeling at all well. Mrs. Hernandez urges her to stay in bed and rest, but Margarita has inherited much of her father's stubbornness. She hurriedly gets ready and leaves for school.

Halfway through her third class, algebra, Margarita can no longer hold her head up. She excuses herself and calls home. Oralia, who has just arrived at the house, comes to get her and drives her home.

Oralia helps her sister change out of her school clothes. Margarita lies down on the bed she shares with Maria.

"Listen, Margarita," Oralia says, "Mami is pretty worried about you, and so am I. She says you hardly touch your food and you're on the phone a lot with your boyfriend. Well, that part is none of my business, but aren't you being a little bit foolish? Think what would happen if you became seriously ill."

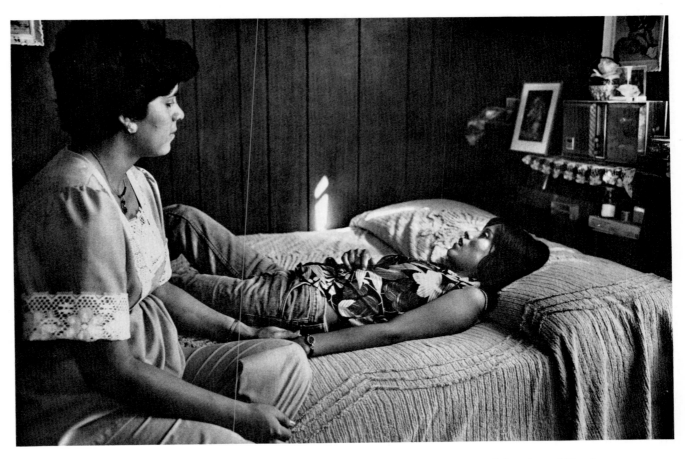

"*Ay*, Oralia," Margarita sighs. "The last thing I want is to give Mami and Papi any troubles. But lately, I'm so confused I don't know what to do."

Margarita is upset about her boyfriend, Ermilio. He is nineteen, a senior at PSJA High, and due to graduate in the spring. But he has been talking about dropping out of school in order to take a full-time job. Margarita has told him that unless he graduates and agrees to go to college for at least two years, they will have to stop seeing each other. Her parents have forbidden Ermilio to visit her at the house, because they think he is being irresponsible about his future. They want their daughters to finish their education before thinking of marriage.

Like Margarita, Florinda, who is seventeen, is a sophomore at PSJA High and attends the afternoon session. Her school day starts at eleven-thirty with a hot lunch in the school cafeteria. As migrant students, she and her sisters are eligible for the free lunch program. For Mrs. Hernandez, the lunch program helps to ease her family's financial burden.

Today's American history class deals with the presidency of John F. Kennedy. Florinda and her classmates are too young to remember those years, and, like many young people, they are more interested in their immediate surroundings and the places in Mexico where their parents were born than in national or world politics. But their teacher remembers the Kennedy years with painful clarity.

The class watches a film about President Kennedy. They listen for the first time to the ringing voice that brought hope to millions of people throughout the world, and they are moved. Then their teacher holds up the front page of a newspaper announcing Kennedy's assassination in Dallas. He is unashamed of the tears in his eyes as he describes the nation's shock and horror on that terrible day. He has given his students much to think about.

The youngest Hernandez daughter, thirteen-year-old Martina, goes to Jefferson Junior High School in Pharr. She is somewhat shy, but is popular with her school-mates. She is also a bright student. She thinks she would like to become either a teacher or a nurse someday.

In Earth Sciences class, the students are given a demonstration of the effects of static electricity. The Van de Graaff generator contains a vertical fan belt that is capped

by a large metallic globe. The belt spins and a steady charge of static electricity is generated in the globe above. When Martina's classmate, Cynthia, places her hands on the globe, she feels a mild shock and nothing more. But the other students are amazed when her hair slowly rises from her head and stands straight up in the air. Her body is acting as a natural conductor for the electric current. Cynthia can't see what's happening, nor does she know until later why the rest of her class was laughing so hard.

Toward the middle of March, Castula Salazar receives a letter from an old uncle in Mexico. He has been in very poor health lately and he misses seeing his relatives who live in Texas. Mrs. Hernandez thinks it would cheer him up if her family were to pay him a visit. On a Sunday after mass, they climb into the van and drive south, into Mexico.

Tio Tomás and his wife live in a *colonia* about two miles from the center of Reynosa. They share one half of a tiny dwelling with another family. They have no electricity or plumbing. Their water must be hauled up in buckets from a communal well.

When Tio Tomás's wife comes to answer the knock on her door, she is overwhelmed with joy and surprise.

"What a pleasure," she says as she warmly embraces each in turn. "Come in, come in. This is your house. You are the best medicine your old uncle could ask for."

Tio Tomás is eighty-two years old. He suffers from severe arthritis. Lately, his feet have been so badly swollen that he has not been able to walk. Although there are drugs that could ease his pain, he cannot afford to buy them.

When the Hernandezes enter, Tio Tomás is lying on his bed. He forces himself into a sitting position.

"Well, and how does it go, Uncle?" asks Mr. Hernandez with concern.

"When I wake up each morning, I thank God for letting me remain here a little bit longer," the old man muses. "But then, as the day wears on, I can't help wondering if He isn't wasting His gift on this useless old body."

36

After a while, Maria and her three younger sisters excuse themselves and go outside. Margarita wanders along the pebbly road to a green, stagnant pond. She tosses small stones into the water and stares at the circular ripples. Hers is a compassionate nature. To witness Tio Tomás's sufferings and not be able to help fills her with distress.

Margarita's reverie is interrupted by a blast from the van's horn. It's time to leave.

Tio Tomás has insisted on walking out to the van to see the Hernandez family off. "Go with God," he says.

"And may it go well with you," responds Mrs. Hernandez, hugging the old man and his wife.

The family wants to do some shopping in Reynosa before going home. The streets are teeming with people. Vendors offer an incredible range of items for sale.

On each street, there are pitiful beggars—some with horrible deformities, others who are merely destitute. All the Hernandez sisters have some painful childhood memories of this place, but they love it anyway.

To Maria, Mexican food has always tasted better on this side of the border, and she can never get enough of it. At the central market of Reynosa, she is finally conquered by the fragrant aromas coming from a taco maker's stall. Here a young man works over an enormous hot pan, stuffing meat, spices, and sauce into freshly made cornmeal tortillas. Maria orders $2 worth—enough to feed the entire family.

Because the family is large and their income is low, they are eligible for food stamps. In fact, they could not manage without them. They pay $80 every month for the stamps that will buy $236 worth of food. Their stamps arrive late this month. It is with a feeling of relief that Mrs. Hernandez finally picks them up at the post office. She asks Maria and Martina to help her do the shopping.

Mrs. Hernandez especially wants to stock up on fresh foods. She knows how important they are to her family's health. Citrus fruit and potatoes sold in bulk are quite cheap here. But although fresh vegetables are produced abundantly in the Valley, most vegetables are costly. And the prices for beef in the Valley are probably the highest in the state of Texas.

Mrs. Hernandez selects eggs and dairy products, frozen fruit juices, and dried and canned goods. In the meat section, she selects a small chicken, some ground beef, and a piece of soup meat. Before long, the shopping cart is full.

The girl at the check-out counter rings up all their purchases. The total is $52.90. Maria looks on glumly as her mother hands over a book of stamps. She wishes her family didn't need this form of assistance in order to eat. But Mrs. Hernandez cannot afford to indulge in wishful thinking.

Saturday night is the one night the Hernandez sisters set aside strictly for having fun. The four younger girls usually go out together. One Saturday in April, Armando Vela calls Mrs. Hernandez to ask if he can take her daughters out bowling in the evening. Armando is a responsible young man who is president of the Legion of Mary chapter of their church. Mrs. Hernandez gives her permission.

The evening starts off happily, but then Margarita calls her boyfriend. She wants him to join her at the bowling alley. Ermilio wants her to go to a dance with him instead. Both refuse to change their plans. When Armando and the girls arrive at the bowling alley, Margarita is in a stormy mood.

Florinda is the first to roll a ball down the alley. *"Ay, caramba,"* she mutters as the ball careens into the gutter. Now she will have to put up with her sisters' teasing.

Next it is Maria's turn. While her sisters chant "We want a strike!" she sets, runs forward, and hurls the ball. To her own amazement, there isn't a pin left standing after the ball connects. "Did you see that?" she cries. "I did it!"

"Beginner's luck," comments Florinda dryly. "Let's see you do it again." But one strike is all that Maria can manage.

As Martina takes her turn, Ermilio suddenly appears. Everyone greets him warmly except Margarita. She is so furious, she refuses even to acknowledge his presence. Ermilio silently accepts her anger and then decides to wait it out.

Armando winds up with the best score. He suggests that they all go to a Dairy Queen for tacos, ice cream, and soft drinks. Maria looks for a way to break the uncomfortable tension between Margarita and her boyfriend. While they wait for their orders, she gets an idea. Grabbing hold of Armando's powerful biceps, she says, "You know, I'll bet you that this *muchacho* thinks he's the strongest man in town. You call this strong? Bah!" she says disdainfully. "Some of my girl friends have stronger muscles. I'll bet even Ermilio has!"

At this, for the first time in the evening, Margarita turns to Ermilio with a smile. Now they can all relax and enjoy one another's company.

46

Early in April, Maria applied for a scholarship to the School of Business Administration at Pan Am University. In May, sooner than she expected, she is notified that she has been awarded scholarship funds to cover tuition, dormitory residence, meals, books, and supplies. She and her family are elated. She will start in the fall.

Just one week later, during the family's Sunday evening meal, Rosa Martha has an announcement to make. She has also been given a scholarship to Pan Am University. Interrupting her sisters' expressions of delight, she points out that her scholarship covers only tuition, books, and supplies. If she accepts it, she will have to quit her job, and that would mean less income for the family. In addition, she would have to begin her classes in June, so she would be unable to go north during the summer. Rosa Martha glances anxiously at her mother.

"Listen, Rosi," Mrs. Hernandez says. "For what other reason have your father and I worked so hard all these years? This is your great opportunity, and you will take it. We have always managed before, and we will manage with this. I know your father will agree."

Later that evening, Mr. Hernandez brings good news. Since February, he has been trying to find summer work for his family. It has been a bitter winter up north and many farming areas will need fewer migrant workers than usual. But, to his relief, he has finally heard of a place where they will be assured of jobs. They will be going to Minnesota to work on a sugar beet farm.

Lazaro is due to come home from the University of Michigan on May 9, and Mrs. Hernandez eagerly looks forward to his arrival. But when there is no sign of him that day, she begins to worry. The next morning, she busies herself with hemming up a pair of her husband's trousers. She is becoming more upset by the minute.

Before he leaves for work, Mr. Hernandez attempts to cheer his wife up. "Try not to worry so much, Maria," he says. "If I know our son, he'll show up when we least expect it."

Sure enough, at a little past six that evening, the screen door creaks open and a tired voice calls out, "Where is everybody?"

Mrs. Hernandez rushes in from the backyard and throws her arms around her son's neck. "Lazaro! Are you all right?" But before he can reply, Lazaro is surrounded by his sisters, all trying to hug and kiss him at the same time.

"Hey! Leave some for me," says Mr. Hernandez, laughing. He welcomes his son with a loving embrace. "*Ay,* it's good to have you back again. I told your mother not to worry about you, but I suppose that is what mothers are for."

Mrs. Hernandez quickly prepares some of the Mexican food her son has missed at school.

While he eats, Lazaro is told about his sisters' scholarships and other current family events. Then he says, "Tell me, Papi, are you going north this summer?"

"Yes," his father replies. "I was lucky—I found work in the sugar beet fields in Minnesota. The man who told me about this has worked there before. He says we can earn good money. Rosa Martha will look after the house while we are up north. That leaves seven of us, but with your strong arms to help, we should do well, don't you think?"

Lazaro's appetite deserts him. "Papi," he says softly, "I won't be able to come with you. I have to make up some credits at Pan Am in order to enter the School of Architecture in the fall."

"Ah," says Mr. Hernandez, unprepared for this news. In one week, he has lost the help of his two oldest and most experienced children. "Well," he adds thoughtfully, "that is equally important. Just the same, we must go, and we will manage."

"But how, Papi?" asks Lazaro. "Are you going to do all the driving from here to Minnesota yourself? Surely you won't let Maria take the wheel on strange roads and at night. And what happens if the van breaks down in the middle of nowhere?"

"We will have the van checked over before we leave. I said we will manage," replies Mr. Hernandez in a tone that does not allow further argument.

During the following week, Lazaro asks an old high school friend, Eduardo de la Rosa, if he will go north with his parents and sisters and work with them in Minnesota. When both Mr. Hernandez and Eduardo agree to the plan, Lazaro is relieved. Lupe Salazar, a young cousin of Lazaro's, volunteers to go along as well. Eduardo and Lupe are both skillful drivers.

With one major concern out of the way, Lazaro next tries to persuade his father to trade in the van for a newer vehicle. To his surprise, his father agrees to look for one. Then, at the used car lot, Lazaro is astonished when Mr. Hernandez picks out not another van but a small car, a 1972 Toyota Corolla. Mr. Hernandez wants Lazaro and Rosa Martha to have transportation to and from Pan Am during the summer.

"But what about the van?" cries Lazaro in frustration.

"I'm taking it to my friend the mechanic this afternoon," says his father. "He'll tell me if there is anything seriously wrong with it. Now, how does this car seem to you? Try it out. If you like it, we have to go and get some financing. We don't have all day, you know."

While his father goes in to see a loan officer at the finance company, Lazaro tells his mother that he is disturbed about the mechanical condition of the van. "Let's forget about buying another car," he says. "I'm just worried about your safety. I honestly don't think the van will be able to make it up north and back. Can't you talk to Papi?"

Mrs. Hernandez listens sympathetically. Then she says gently, "You know your father would never put us in danger. Trust him. Besides, in this matter I happen to agree with him."

The price of the used Toyota is $890. Lazaro wants to make the monthly payments on the auto loan. They will be $80 a month for one year—a total of $960. His father says he will go along with Lazaro's proposal for the summer months, and signs the loan agreement.

Saturday, May 27, is a busy day for the Hernandez family. They will be leaving for Minnesota sometime the next day. Mr. Hernandez has gone to pick up the van, which has been looked over and lubricated. Lazaro and Rosa Martha have gone to Pan Am University to register for their summer courses. And tonight, Maria will graduate from high school.

In the afternoon, Mr. Hernandez comes home tired and decides to take a nap. Soon after, Oralia arrives at the house. With their father safely out of the way, the girls quickly hustle their mother into their front bedroom and close the door. Mrs. Hernandez wants to have her hair cut.

"Maybe we'd better not cut it too short," suggests Oralia. "Papi will be furious."

"Does he think I'm going to work in the fields under a hot sun with all this weight on my head?" replies Mrs. Hernandez. "But maybe you're right. We don't want him in a bad mood for Maria's graduation. Cut a little off now and we'll cut it some more tomorrow."

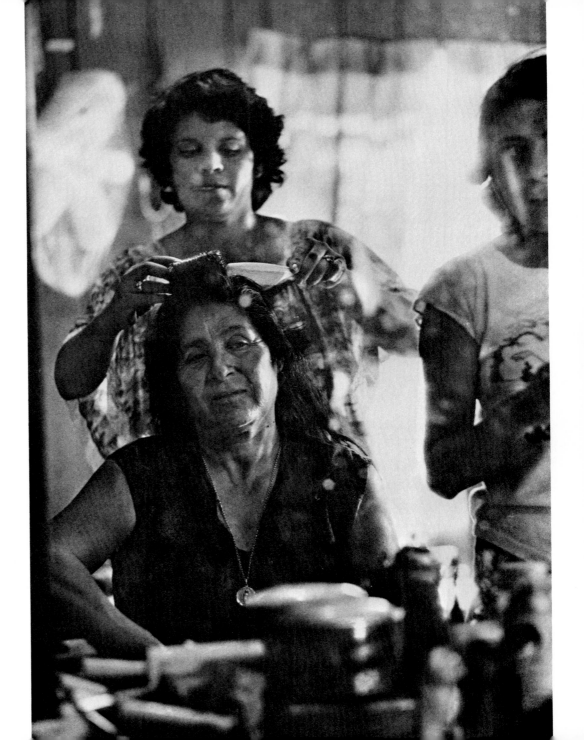

Margarita contentedly applies polish to her fingernails. She is feeling more optimistic about life. Ermilio recently had a serious talk with her parents. He told them he had decided to graduate from high school and go on to college in the fall. He assured them that he would not interfere with Margarita's education and that his intentions toward her were serious and honorable. Mr. and Mrs. Hernandez were impressed with his sincerity and wished him success.

Maria slips into her white graduation dress and combs out her hair. She is due at the high school stadium at six P.M. The ceremonies will begin at eight, but time must be allowed for the eager and excited students to gather and organize so that things will go smoothly. This is a very important ceremony to Maria and her friends. It marks both a significant achievement and the promise of bright futures.

For once, there are no teasing comments from her sisters when Maria has finished dressing—only compliments. Maria warns her parents that they too should arrive early, if they hope to find enough space for the family to sit together.

On her way to the stadium, Maria goes over the details of the ceremony in her mind. The PSJA band will strike up a stately march, and the students will walk onto the field and take seats reserved for them. There will be speeches from community leaders, and then the class will go up one by one to receive their diplomas.

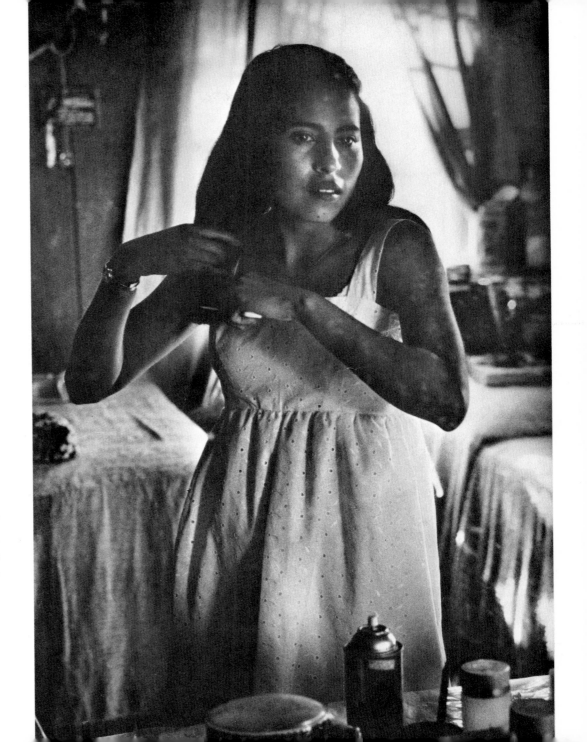

A velvety darkness has fallen over the large assembly. The lights are turned on. The ceremony is under way.

"Maria Hernandez."

With a radiant smile, Maria walks through the garlanded archway and shakes the hand of the official who gives her her diploma. After the last one has been awarded, the graduates join hands and sing the school song for the last time. Mr. McKeever, the principal, proudly announces, "I now declare this class officially graduated."

Wild cheers break out all over the stadium as the students toss their graduation caps into the air. This will be a special night of celebration.

The following morning, right after mass, the Hernandezes start packing for their journey north. Maria and her sisters have migrated every year since they were very small girls. They know from experience what to take and what to leave behind. There will be few opportunities for fun and recreation, so they pack only old, sturdy, comfortable work clothing. Although Mr. Hernandez grumbles, his wife has her daughters cut her hair quite short.

After lunch, Maria drives her mother to a supermarket where they shop for staple provisions. Up north, some items will be far more costly than they are here. Others may not be available at all. Mrs. Hernandez buys a twenty-five-pound bag of cornmeal for making tortillas, tamales, and enchiladas. She hopes it will be enough for the eight people she will have to cook for. She also stocks up on pinto beans, an inexpensive, high-protein food that is an important part of any Mexican meal.

Late in the afternoon, Mr. and Mrs. Hernandez sit down to work out their finances and discuss what lies ahead. Mr. Hernandez spreads out a large road map of the United States on the kitchen table and tries to trace the route they will follow. The sugar beet farm is near Halstad, Minnesota, but he can't locate it on the map. They will be driving behind a Mr. Alvarez, who, with his family, has worked on that farm for the past sixteen summers.

Now they must finish the packing. The food is securely fastened in large gunny-sacks. Towels, blankets, bedding, and cooking utensils are packed. They don't want to take too much, but they don't know what their living conditions will be like in Minnesota, and it is best to be reasonably prepared.

In the evening, Lazaro and Eduardo work anxiously under the hood of the van. They find and repair leaks in the water and oil lines. Then they carefully check the air pressure in the tires, and inspect them for damage. Lazaro has done everything he can to make sure the van will be safe.

At midnight, with the help of Lazaro, Eduardo, and Lupe, Mr. Hernandez loads up the van. There is a clear space behind the last seat in the rear that measures about four by five feet. All the trunks and sacks are wedged in here to provide an even surface. An old mattress and some blankets are placed on top to serve as a makeshift bed.

There is nothing more to do except wait for Mr. Alvarez. The house is strangely subdued. All the good-byes have been said but two, and these are the hardest of all to say. It is the first time that Rosa Martha and Lazaro will not accompany the family on their annual migration north.

It is two-thirty in the morning when Mr. Alvarez arrives. The Hernandezes quickly climb into the van. Eduardo gets behind the wheel. Soon they are speeding through the darkness behind Mr. Alvarez's converted pickup.

For a while, there is animated conversation as everyone speculates on how long it will take them to get to Minnesota. But by the time the van pulls into a gas station for refueling, Martina and Florinda are fast asleep in the back. And not long after that, only Mr. and Mrs. Hernandez remain awake to keep their young driver company.

As daylight filters through the windows, Mrs. Hernandez and her daughters, bleary-eyed, peer outside. A watery sun rises over the Texas landscape.

By noon, it has become a sweltering day. The temperature outside is in the upper nineties. With the sun beating down on the roof, it is well over one hundred degrees inside the van, although it is moving fast and all the windows are wide open.

62

Everyone is thirsty. Mrs. Hernandez has brought along a cold-storage container with cans of soft drink packed in ice. These quickly vanish, and they will not be replaced until the next stop at a gas station.

Mr. Hernandez and Mr. Alvarez have agreed to try to lose as little time on the road as they can. As a result, stops are infrequent and brief, allowing only enough time to refuel while everyone scrambles for the rest rooms.

Shortly after three in the afternoon, the van leaves Texas and enters Oklahoma. Lupe now takes his turn as driver. Though the supply of food they packed for the road is running out, the Hernandezes have no desire to stop and replenish it here. They have long memories. Only a few years ago, diners and roadside cafés throughout this territory hung up signs that read, "NO MEXICANS OR DOGS ALLOWED." Even today, during their brief refueling stops, their money is taken sullenly and with stony-eyed stares.

They cross the state line into Kansas at eight-thirty P.M. Half an hour later, ominous black clouds descend over the highway. Suddenly the temperature plunges to below fifty degrees. The skies let loose a deluge of driving rain, while gigantic bolts of lightning explode around them with frightening intensity. It takes all of Mr. Hernandez's strength to control the van as it is buffeted by fierce winds. Eduardo turns the radio on; there is a major tornado alert. After a tense hour, the storm lets up as abruptly as it began.

By ten o'clock, all the restaurants and diners along the highway have closed for the night. Cold and hungry, Maria and Margarita share the sleeping space in the back of the van. Tonight it is Florinda's and Martina's turn to make do on one of the seats, huddling together for warmth. Soon everyone but Eduardo is asleep. He drives through the night with the radio loudly blaring rock music to keep him awake.

At five o'clock on Tuesday morning, they stop for breakfast at an all-night restaurant in Nebraska. The service is friendly, the food is delicious, and the hot, fragrant coffee keeps on coming. When they clamber back into the van, everybody feels refreshed.

It looks like a perfect day for driving—breezy, dry, and comfortably warm.

Mrs. Hernandez is entranced by the Nebraskan landscape they are speeding through. "How like a woman," she murmurs, admiring the softly curving contours of the fertile land.

"Yes," agrees Margarita, laughing, "and a very neat woman, too. She doesn't have a pin out of place."

Something is wrong with the van's brakes. Instead of stopping promptly when Mr. Hernandez presses his foot on the pedal, the van continues to move forward for a few yards. This could be dangerous. Mr. Hernandez blows his horn as a signal for Mr. Alvarez to pull into a gas station and garage down the road.

Mrs. Hernandez decides to call home while a mechanic checks out the brakes. Margarita dials the long-distance operator, who puts through the call to Pharr. When Rosa Martha answers the phone, Margarita notices something strange in her sister's voice.

"What's the matter?" she asks suspiciously.

As the reluctant reply comes over the wire, Margarita presses her hand to her face in shock and sorrow. One of her father's favorite uncles in Mexico has just died.

After an hour and a half, the mechanic has only managed to tighten the brakes as a stopgap measure. The parts are badly worn and need to be replaced. But this is not possible—the van would be out of commission for days. With each hour on the road their cash reserves dwindle, and each day's delay in reaching their destination means a reduction in their summer's income. Mr. Hernandez pays the bill and thanks the mechanic for his help.

As they continue their journey north, the mood in the van is somber. By nine P.M. they have left Nebraska, passed through South Dakota, and are entering North Dakota. With Lupe asleep beside him, Mr. Hernandez, pushing aside his grief over his uncle, remains stubbornly awake, his eyes fixed on the road over Eduardo's shoulder.

He is impatient to get the trip over with so that they can begin to work. Mrs. Hernandez is worried about what they may find at the farm where they will stay.

Night has fallen on the second day of their journey. At ten o'clock, they enter the state of Minnesota. Two hours later, they turn off the main highway past the town of Halstad onto a secondary road. In a few minutes, under the light of a full moon, the white forms of farm buildings loom out of the darkness. They have arrived.

Eduardo turns the van into a dirt lane. On rubbery legs, the weary travelers climb out onto firm ground to look at their new surroundings. On one side of them is a row of small, one-room houses where the single men will bunk. On the other side is a long building divided into large rooms for families.

Mrs. Hernandez is eager to explore their living quarters. Opening a screen door, she enters a freshly painted room with an exposed concrete floor. In one corner there is a kitchen with a gas stove, a sink, and a good-sized refrigerator; next to this stands a large table flanked by two long benches. There are shelves on the walls. At the far end of the room are two iron, double bed frames with mattresses. Everything is spotlessly clean. "Thank God," sighs Mrs. Hernandez with relief. "We will not live in a pigpen." She vividly remembers the awful living conditions her family encountered when they began migrating.

Everyone springs into action, and in fifteen minutes the van is unloaded. The girls find places for all of the trunks and family possessions while their mother puts together a makeshift meal.

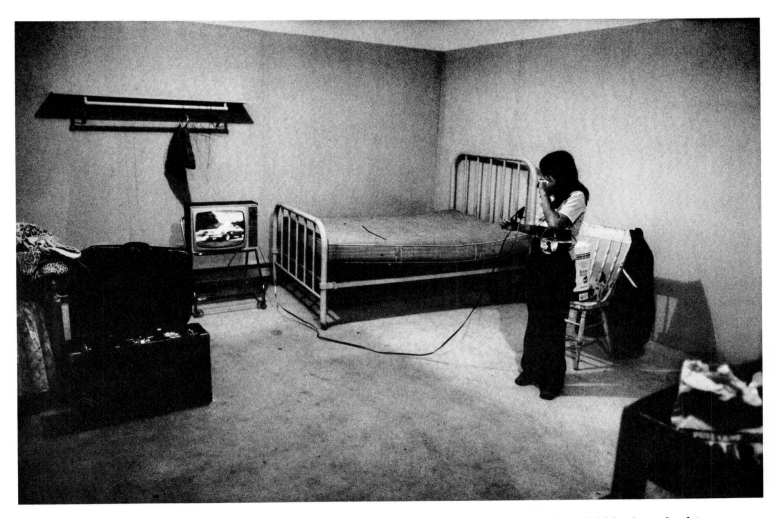

"Look, Mami," calls Margarita excitedly. She has discovered an old black-and-white TV set. She can hardly wait to see if it works. Nervously chewing her thumbnail, she fiddles around with the set's dials and antenna until she gets a fairly decent picture.

Mr. and Mrs. Hernandez will sleep in one of the beds, Martina and Florinda will share the other. The mattress from the back of the van is placed on the floor. This is where Maria and Margarita will sleep tonight. They are far too tired to mind.

The next day is devoted to getting settled in. Eduardo and Lupe occupy one of the small houses opposite the Hernandezes' room. They have an extra bed that they bring over for the Hernandez sisters. Maria and Margarita carry the heavy mattress across the lane. Now, no one will have to sleep on the floor.

Mrs. Hernandez and Margarita have organized the kitchen. Together they prepare their first hot meal—fresh tortillas, beans, potatoes with onions, and coffee. Mrs. Hernandez has brought along a jar of her wonderful homemade chili sauce. Already this place is beginning to smell a little bit like home.

While the girls unpack, their parents have a serious discussion about finances. They have spent more than $200 for gas, food, supplies, and car repairs over the past two days. They have very little money left. Only $85 worth of food stamps remain of their month's allotment.

"We must find out if we can get food stamps while we are here," says Mr. Hernandez unhappily. Having just arrived, he doesn't want to bother the farmer with a request for assistance.

Mr. Alvarez comes in with a young man whom he introduces as Mr. Sing. Mr. Sing is the field agricultural man for the American Crystal Sugar Company, the company that will buy the farmer's sugar beet crop. It is his job to see that the migrant workers in this county get fair treatment and decent living conditions. Mr. Hernandez quickly assures him that they are pleased with their quarters and eager to work.

"Well," says Mr. Alvarez, laughing, "you'll get plenty of that here, believe me."

"Yes, and I think you'll find the farmer a good man to work for," adds Mr. Sing.

Mr. Sing explains that Mr. Hernandez's group will be paid the same wages that Mr. Alvarez receives—$26 per acre. The more acres they cover, the more they will earn. They will be paid when they have finished their work and are ready to return home.

"Please call me if you need any help, any time," says Mr. Sing as he leaves his card.

The family drives to the nearby town of Ada. At the county courthouse they register a certificate for food stamps, but there will be a delay. The permanent residents in this area don't use the food stamp program, so the county is not set up to handle applications efficiently.

Mrs. Hernandez goes to a supermarket and uses some of their precious stamps to buy some meat, milk, and fresh vegetables. Then she goes to the post office. Out of their remaining funds, she purchases a $20 money order and sends it by air mail to Mexico. It will help pay for their uncle's funeral.

At five o'clock the next morning, Mr. Hernandez awakens his daughters, Eduardo, and Lupe. By seven o'clock the Hernandez sisters are scrambling down a grassy knoll behind their father, hoes in hand, ready for their first day's work.

Five hundred of the farm's five thousand acres are planted with sugar beets. Their job will be to thin the sugar beet plants and cut the weeds around them with their hoes.

They must estimate how much space should remain between plants and decide which plants to clean out and which to leave. Spacing the plants will allow the sugar beets to grow to their maximum size and thus yield maximum profit when the crop is sold to the sugar company. In another four weeks, this same field will require a meticulous final cutting of all the weeds.

Since they have not done this job before, Mr. Alvarez works the first row of plants ahead of them so they can follow his example.

Soon the girls fall into the rhythm of the work. The pace is slow. The field they are working in is half a mile long; it takes them forty-five minutes to clean one row of plants. But after a few hours, they feel confident that they can handle the work.

78

At noon, they break for a hot lunch that Mrs. Hernandez has prepared. The warmth of the food is especially welcome because they are unused to the cool weather this far north.

Mr. Hernandez quickly urges them back to work. He doesn't like the look of the sky. If it should rain hard, all work in the fields would have to stop.

With each passing hour, the girls' hoes grow heavier in their hands. Their arms, shoulders, and backs develop a dull, steady ache. Finally, at six o'clock, Mr. Hernandez says they have done enough for today. They have worked ten hours. Sighing with relief, the girls trudge wearily back to their room.

Right after dinner, Margarita is ready for bed. Martina joins her. She is worried about her sister. "Is something wrong?" she asks. "Are you feeling sick?"

"It's nothing," Margarita whispers. "Don't worry, I'm just tired, that's all."

As one day succeeds another, the work never varies. The farmer has arranged credit for the Hernandezes at Halstad's single, small grocery shop, but the food they buy there costs almost four times as much as the food they could buy with food stamps at the supermarket in Ada. And now the van's brakes have stopped functioning. Mr. Hernandez has left the van in town to have the worn brake parts replaced. In spite of their reluctance to impose on him, they must rely on Mr. Alvarez for transportation.

Mrs. Hernandez works in the fields every day along with the rest of her family. She treats the sugar beet plants with the same care and respect that she lavishes on her garden at home.

Although her pregnancy is advanced, Mrs. Alvarez stubbornly insists on helping her family in the fields as well.

At first, each woman views the other's family with polite caution. With three handsome Alvarez boys and four pretty Hernandez girls living in such close proximity, both mothers fear some mischief. But when they see that the boys treat the girls with respect and courtesy, and that the girls are friendly but keep their distance, the women relax and become good neighbors.

Hardly a day goes by without light showers. Even when the ground is dry, it isn't easy to walk between the rows of sugar beet plants. The rain makes the fields increasingly mucky to work in. The girls stop often to scrape mud off their hoe blades and sharpen the dulled edges with steel files. Because their work is slowed, they must put in extra hours to cover the same acreage they would in dry weather.

At seven in the evening, the Hernandez sisters climb onto the rear of the Alvarez pickup, ready to return to their quarters. Martina is drooping with fatigue, too tired to respond to Maria's concerned comments. Margarita surveys the blisters on her hands and the ragged state of her fingernails with silent resignation.

After they have bathed and changed, the girls help their mother prepare dinner. The aroma of familiar foods and the warm sound of their mother's voice calms and comforts them. Somehow, their aches and pains don't seem so bad anymore.

At the end of each day, Mr. Alvarez comes to talk with Mr. Hernandez. He is in charge of the daily work tally book, in which he records the number of acres they have covered. So far, the Hernandezes have averaged four and a half acres a day. At $26 per acre, this amounts to $117 a day. Mr. Alvarez says that last year, he and his family earned $6,000 on the farm. He believes that because they have more people working, the Hernandez group should be able to earn even more than that by the end of the summer. This is encouraging news.

It rains on and off all the next day. Nevertheless, work continues in the fields. At four o'clock, there is a loud clap of thunder and the rain comes down in torrents. The ground quickly turns into slippery mud.

When the family gets back to their quarters, they are sopping wet and laughing at their bedraggled appearance. Mr. Hernandez strips off his soaked undershirt. His wife brings him a fresh one. He had planned to work until seven tonight. Now, if the rain continues, there may be no work at all tomorrow.

An hour later, the rain stops abruptly, the clouds vanish, and there is brilliant, warm sunshine. While Mrs. Hernandez takes a load of laundry to the washing ma-

chine in the women's bathroom, Martina sweeps the floor free of caked mud. Margarita opens the curtains to let more sun into the room and then helps Maria fix dinner.

Mr. Hernandez takes a kitchen knife and punches a wide slot in the top of a beer can. Then, fishing in his pockets for loose change, he drops coins into the can one by one. "They say a few coins a day helps keep the rain away."

"You and your 'they say,' Papi," teases Maria as she mashes the refried beans for dinner. "Have you heard this one? They say that a meal without beans is like eating thin air."

"Don't try to pull this coyote's tail," growls her father with mock severity. "You are speaking to the man who *invented* that one."

Nine-year-old Maribel Alvarez and her little brother Genaro come to visit the sisters after dinner. Florinda, rummaging around in a trunk, brings out a game of

chance, which she sets up on the kitchen table. Soon there are five happy players excitedly waiting their turns to win play money.

While her younger sisters play with the Alvarez children, Maria settles down to write letters to cousins and friends back in Texas. This is the first chance she has had to do anything like this since the family arrived in Minnesota.

Later in the evening, Mr. Alvarez brings disturbing news. Because of the unstable weather, the farmer is afraid that his sugar beet fields may not be adequately thinned and weeded in time for harvesting. He has sent for another migrant family to come and help speed up the work. With more people in the fields, there will be less work for the Hernandez group and, therefore, less money for all when they are done. Now, no matter how hard they work, it will be impossible to make as much money as they had hoped. Mr. Hernandez does not blame the farmer. He knows that he is a hardworking, fair-minded man

who must solve his own problems as best he can. Besides, only God can control the weather.

At the beginning of their third week, the family's food stamps arrive. By now the preliminary thinning and weeding of the sugar beets is finished; the plants have begun to mature. It is time for the final weeding.

By the end of their fourth week, all work in the beet fields has been completed.
There is nothing more for the Hernandez family to do.

It's time to start packing for the trip home, but Margarita is too tired to move.

"Margarita," Florinda calls, "are you going home with us or not? Maybe we should just roll you up in that blanket and pack you as extra bedding for the trip. Or, if you like, we'll leave you here. I'm sure Ermilio won't mind if you don't come home."

Margarita revives at the mention of Ermilio's name. She flashes her sister a good-natured grin and starts to help with the packing.

The farmer has been happy with the Hernandezes' work and has invited them to return next year. He has also offered them the continued use of their living quarters if they wish to seek other employment in the area now.

"What do you think, Maria?" Mr. Hernandez asks his wife. "Perhaps we should stay and look for more work."

"Who knows how long it may take to get new work, or how much money we will have to spend while we're looking?" his wife replies. "Let's take the money we have earned and go home now. Maybe next summer we will have better luck."

"All right," says Mr. Hernandez. "Tomorrow I will cash our check at the bank in town and we will pay all our debts. We will go home the following day."

On the way back to Texas, Mrs. Hernandez completes a final accounting of their assets. For their month's work, they have received a total of $3,800, not counting Lupe's and Eduardo's earnings. After paying for gas, food, and all other expenses, they are left with less than $2,500.

Mrs. Hernandez reads out her calculations to her husband. "We have come so far for so little," she says, sighing. "It will be a difficult year."

Affectionately squeezing his wife's shoulder, David Hernandez replies, "We will manage, Maria. Don't worry. We will manage."

Four days later, when they arrive in the Rio Grande Valley, the temperature is over one hundred degrees. To those inside the Hernandez van, the heat is a welcome, familiar tonic. They are only ten miles from home.

In this proud land there are many Americas. There is an America of inequality and racial prejudice. There is an America of grave poverty, despair, and tragic human waste. And yet, because of people like the Hernandez family, there is also an America of simple courage, strength, and hope.